TWINKLE, TWII
PLANET BLU

An astronaut high in the sky,
Looked down on the Earth with a sigh.
He wept for the lost trees
And fish dead in the seas,
And waved the old planet goodbye.

Jackie Murphy

Cambridge Reading

General Editors
Richard Brown and Kate Ruttle

Consultant Editor
Jean Glasberg

PUBLISHED BY THE PRESS SYNDICATE OF THE UNIVERSITY OF CAMBRIDGE
The Pitt Building, Trumpington Street, Cambridge CB2 1RP, United Kingdom

CAMBRIDGE UNIVERSITY PRESS
The Edinburgh Building, Cambridge CB2 2RU, United Kingdom
40 West 20th Street, New York, NY 10011-4211, USA
10 Stamford Road, Oakleigh, Melbourne 3166, Australia

First published 1998

Printed in the United Kingdom at the University Press, Cambridge

Typeset in Concorde

A catalogue record for this book is available from the British Library

ISBN 0 521 55558 2 paperback

Twinkle, Twinkle, Planet Blue

Selected by Morag Styles

Illustrated by Mario Minichiello

CAMBRIDGE
UNIVERSITY PRESS

**Other Cambridge Reading books
you may enjoy**

The Hermit Shell
Frances Usher

In the Court of the Jade Emperor
Rosalind Kerven

Whisked Away
Richard Brown

**Other books by Morag Styles
you may enjoy**

By the Pricking of My Thumbs

Dream Time

My Brother's a Beast

Contents

Morning Has Broken

Birdsong, Leaves and Sky

I Love the Rain

Twinkle, Twinkle, Planet Blue

All You Sea

I Sing for the Animals

Extinction Day

Enjoy the Earth Gently

Morning Has Broken

Morning Has Broken

Morning has broken . . .
Too late the billion gallons of sun lotion
Smeared over the earth's surface
The straw hat covering three continents
Too late the sunglasses wrapped around the equator
The giant space parasol
Too late the ozone elastoplast

Morning has broken . . .
Is it too late to mend it?

Roger McGough

I Won't Hatch!

Oh I am a chickie who lives in an egg,
But I will not hatch, I will not hatch.
The hens they all cackle, the roosters all beg,
But I will not hatch, I will not hatch.
For I hear all the talk of pollution and war
As the people all shout and the airplanes all roar,
So I'm staying in here where it's safe and it's warm,
And I will not hatch!

Shel Silverstein

Harvest Hymn

We plough the fields and scatter
our pesticides again;
our seeds are fed and watered
by gentle acid rain.
We spray the corn in winter
till pests and weeds are dead –
who minds a little poison
inside his daily bread?

All good gifts around us
beneath our ozone layer
are safe, oh Lord,
so thank you Lord
that we know how to care.

Judith Nicholls

Song of the City

My brain is stiff with concrete
My limbs are rods of steel
My belly's stuffed with money
My soul was bought in a deal.

They poured metal through my arteries
They choked my lungs with lead
They churned my blood to plastic
They put murder into my head.

I'd a face like a map of the weather
Flesh that grew to the bone
But they tore my story out of my eyes
And turned my heart to stone.

Let me wind from my source like a river
Let me grow like wheat from the grain
Let me hold out my arms like a natural tree
Let my children love me again.

Gareth Owen

Landscape

What will you find at the edge of the world?
A footprint,
a feather,
desert sand swirled?
A tree of ice,
a rain of stars,
or a junkyard of cars?

What will there be at the rim of the earth?
A mollusc,
a mammal,
a new creature's birth?
Eternal sunrise,
immortal sleep,
or cars piled up in a rusty heap?

Eve Merriam

I Have an Oasis

I have an oasis,
It's up in the clouds
Away from the rush
And the roar of the crowds,
Away from the pushing
And pulling and pain,
Away from the sadness
And anger and strain,
Away from the envy
And cheating and greed,
Away from the pressure –
What more could I need?
I grow my geraniums
And lettuce that's curled,
In my little garden
On top of the world.

Colin McNaughton

I had a little piece of earth,
Nothing would it grow
But a tangled crop of weeds,
Sunshine, rain or snow.

My granny and her sack of tools
Came to visit me,
So now I've got a bed of blooms
And one small apple tree.

Lucy Coates

The Village Shop

Push the door. Ssh! Don't tell.
Listen to the old shop bell.
Imagine what they used to sell
Fifty years ago –

Gobstoppers and Cherry-lips,
Humbugs, Sherbet, Lemon Pips
in little pointed paper slips.

Home from school, to the shop,
Beano, butter, lemon pop,
papers, stamps, ring-ring, non-stop
Yesterday.

Flip-flops, knickers, Pogs and wellies,
String and bottle gas and jelly,
Sugar, carrots, vermicelli.

Now we drive to the supermarket.
Fumes and traffic. Stop and park it.
Fill the trolley. Pay by credit.

No more running down the street
when we run out of milk. No treats.
No kind hand with extra sweets.

No shop. No school. No bus. No train.
No quiet little country lanes.
Just fumes and ozone in the air
and hurry, hurry everywhere.

Gillian Clarke

Raw Food

Harrybo's dad grows hundreds of vegetables
and Harrybo says:
'Let's go down the garden . . .'
and he attacks his dad's broad beans.
'Come on, you have some,' he says,
and he's munching through five of them.
I don't like them very much.
Maybe I'll just have one
to show I'm not feeble.

Then he goes for the peas.
'These are GREAT,' he says,
'really sweet.'
And he sticks his thumb in the pod
and squirts a row of raw peas into his mouth.

Sometimes he pulls up radishes and carrots,
wipes the mud off them
bites the tops off
and munches up the rest.

'You want to try potatoes, Michael,' he says,
and he heaves one of his dad's potatoes up,
wipes the mud off that too
and –
crunch –
he eats a raw potato
then
red currants
black currants
gooseberries.

I once said the red currants
smelt like cat's pee.
Didn't bother him.
He gobbles these till his chin
runs red.

And the apples.
His dad grows the hardest, bitterest apples
you've ever seen,
with knobbly, leathery skins.

'Great!' says Harrybo,
'let's get at the apples.'
And he munches them up:
the whole thing –
the core
the pips
the little hairy bits at the ends.
He leaves nothing.

He even found some little green pip things.
'Stursham seeds', he called them.
'Try these,' he says.
They were sour, peppery beans.
Horrible.
'I love these,' he said
and he scooped handfuls of them into his mouth.

It's incredible watching him
roaming round the garden
grabbing at anything growing.
He chews grass.
He eats dandelion leaves.
'These are just great, Michael,' he says.
'*You* ought to eat them, you know.'

I've seen people very carefully nibbling at
one raw mushroom
thinking they're doing something
daringly healthy.

Harrybo can munch up twenty.

Michael Rosen

Birdsong, Leaves and Sky

Haiku Moment

Stopped here listening –
this heedless grind of traffic
staggers the birdsongs.

James Berry

Conceit

I heard a winter tree in song.
Its leaves were birds, a hundred strong;
When all at once it ceased to sing
For every leaf had taken wing.

Mervyn Peake

Felled Trees

Nobody has come to burn them,
Long green grass grows up between them,
Up between white boughs that lie
Dead and empty, dry,
That once were full of leaves and sky.

Ruth Dallas

The Prayer of the Little Bird

Dear God,
I don't know how to pray by myself
very well,
but will You please
protect my little nest from wind and rain?
Put a great deal of dew on the flowers,
many seeds in my way.
Make Your blue very high,
Your branches lissom;
let Your kind light stay late in the sky
and set my heart brimming with such music
that I must sing, sing, sing . . .
Please, Lord.

Carmen Bernos de Gasztold
translated by Rumer Godden

Be Like the Bird

Be like the bird, who
Resting in his flight
On a twig too slight
Feels it bend beneath him,
Yet sings
Knowing he has wings.

Victor Hugo

Thrush

The speckled Thrush
With a cheerful shout
Dips his beak in the dark
And lifts the sun out.

Then he calls to the Snails:
'God's here again!
Close your eyes for prayers
While I sing Amen.

And after Amen
Rejoice! Rejoice!'

Then he scoops up some dew
and washes his voice.

Ted Hughes

Words

In woods are words.
You hear them all,
Winsome, witless or wise,
When the birds call.

In woods are words.
If your ears wake
You hear them, quiet and clear,
When the leaves shake.

In woods are words.
You hear them all
Blown by the wet wind
When raindrops fall.

In woods are words
Kind or unkind;
Birds, leaves and hushing rain
Bring them to mind.

James Reeves

Trees Are Great

Trees are great, they just stand and wait
They don't cry when they're teased
They don't eat much and they seldom shout
Trees are easily pleased

Trees are great, they like to congregate
For meetings in the park
They dance and sway, they stay all day
And talk till well after dark

Trees are great, they accept their fate
When it's pouring down with rain
They don't wear macs, it runs off their backs
But you never hear them complain

So answer me, please, if there weren't any trees
Where would naughty boys climb?
Where would lovers carve their names?
Where would little birds nest?
Where would we hang the leaves?

Roger McGough

Autumn Sigheth

Wind bloweth,
Water floweth
Feather flieth,
Bird goeth.
Whither, bird?
Who can tell?
None knoweth . . .
Farewell.

Wind bawleth,
Summer palleth,
Rose fadeth,
Leaf falleth.
Wither, leaf.
Where you fell,
Winter calleth . . .
Farewell.

Tree turneth,
Bonfire burneth,
Earth resteth,
Sleep earneth.
Whither, earth?
To dream a spell
Till flower returneth . . .
Sleep well.

Eleanor Farjeon

Pine Forest

The track cuts through the forest
Like a parting. Between the trees
It's dark, a place for gnomes
And goblins. Near the ground
A snow of grey-white fungus
Lives on leafless wood.

'Just a little way,' you say
'Along this path.' Pine needles
Inches deep, an island of fresh grass
Where there is sun. We're whispering
As if we were in church.
Ahead of us the tunnel reaches
into blackness. I take your hand.

Wendy Cope

The Rainflower

Down in the forest where light never falls
There's a place that no one else knows,
A deep marshy hollow beside a grey lake
And that's where the rainflower grows.

The one silver rainflower that's left in the world,
Alone in the mist and the damp,
Lifts up its bright head from a cluster of leaves
And shines through the gloom like a lamp.

Far from the footpaths and far from the roads,
In a silence where no birds call,
It blooms like a secret, a star in all the dark,
The last silver rainflower of all.

So keep close behind me and follow me down,
I'll take you where no one else goes,
And there in the hollow beside the grey lake,
We'll stand where the rainflower grows.

Richard Edwards

The Way through the Woods

They shut the road through the woods
   Seventy years ago.
Weather and rain have undone it again,
   And now you would never know
There was once a road through the woods
   Before they planted the trees.

It is underneath the coppice and heath,
   And the thin anemones.
   Only the keeper sees
That, where the ring-dove broods,
   And the badgers roll at ease,
There was once a road through the woods.

Yet, if you enter the woods
   Of a summer evening late,
When the night-air cools on the trout-ringed pools
   Where the otter whistles his mate,
(They fear not men in the woods,
   Because they see so few)
You will hear the beat of a horse's feet
   And the swish of a skirt in the dew,
   Steadily cantering through
The misty solitudes,
   As though they perfectly knew
The old lost road through the woods . . .
But there is no road through the woods.

Rudyard Kipling

Oxleas Wood

I have adopted a tree
with my own pocket money.
It only cost me
a fiver for that old oak tree –
it is older than a century.

They are trying to build a motorway
through this magic mystery,
this ancient wise wood.

Whose will is done?
Who will let them?

They are trying to build a motorway
through this magic mystery,
this ancient wise wood.

We will wait for the bulldozers to come.
We will all lie down.
We won't let our children be chopped down.
We will all lie down.
We are the children who won't let our children go.
We are the parents who must lie down.
To fight for the ozone layer, the future.
The bark, the leaf, the branch, the air.
We will not be moved.

Jackie Kay

For Forest

Forest could keep secrets
Forest could keep secrets

Forest tune in every day
to watersound and birdsong
Forest letting her hair down
to the teeming creeping of her forest-ground

But forest don't broadcast her business
no Forest cover her business down
from sky and fast-eye sun
and when night come
and darkness wrap her like a gown
Forest is a bad dream woman

Forest dreaming about mountain
and when earth was young
Forest dreaming of the caress of gold
Forest rootsing with mysterious Eldorado

and when howler monkey
wake her up with howl
Forest just stretch and stir
to a new day of sound

but coming back to secrets
Forest could keep secrets
Forest could keep secrets

And we must keep Forest

Grace Nichols

I Love the Rain

The Dry Season

The year is withering; the wind
Blows down the leaves;
Men stand under eaves
And overhear the secrets
Of the cold dry wind,
Of the half-bare trees.

The grasses are tall and tinted,
Straw-gold hues of dryness,
And the contradicting awryness,
Of the dusty roads a-scatter
With the pools of colourful leaves,
With ghosts of the dreaming year.

And soon, soon the fires,
The fires will begin to burn,
The hawk will flutter and turn
On its wings and swoop for the mouse,
The dogs will run for the hare,
The hare for its little life.

Kwesi Brew

Thunderstorm in the Fourth Dry Summer

Clouds hurled their silver spears
With a sound of thunder
But earth had hardened her shield
In fires of the sun.
Only the trees,
Dusty, weary and drying,
Clapped feeble hands
And pitifully cried for more.

Nan Hunt

The Whisper

Around the world the whisper goes,
A gentle, universal breath,
And everything that hears it grows.

At its command the river flows,
A blade of light, a glittering sheath –
Around the world the whisper goes.

What it is saying no one knows
Although it tells of life not death
And everything that hears it grows.

It takes the measure of its foes,
It makes a garland of a wreath –
Around the world the whisper goes.

It fills with hope the wind that blows
Across the desolated heath
And everything that hears it grows.

Above us all it still bestows
A blessing on what lies beneath.
Around the world the whisper goes
And everything that hears it grows.

John Mole

An Aboriginal Simile

There was no stir among the trees,
No pulse in the earth,
No movement in the void;
The grass was a dry white fire.
Then in the distance rose a cloud,
And a swift rain came:
Like a woman running,
The wind in her hair.

Mary Gilmore

April Rain Song

Let the rain kiss you.
Let the rain beat upon your head with silver liquid drops.
Let the rain sing you a lullaby.

The rain makes still pools on the sidewalk.
The rain makes running pools in the gutter.
The rain plays a little sleep-song on our roof at night –

And I love the rain.

Langston Hughes

A Song for England

An' a so de rain a-fall
An' a so de snow a-rain

An' a so de fog a-fall
An' a so de sun a-fail

An' a so de seasons mix
An' a so de bag-o'-tricks

But a so me understan'
De misery o'de Englishman.

Andrew Salkey

Up in the Morning Early

Cauld blaws the wind frae east to west,
The drift is driving sairly;
Sae loud and shrill's I hear the blast,
I'm sure it's winter fairly.

Up in the morning's no for me,
Up in the morning early;
When a' the hills are cover'd wi' snaw,
I'm sure it's winter fairly.

The birds sit chittering in the thorn,
A' day they fare but sparely;
And lang's the night frae e'en to morn,
I'm sure it's winter fairly.

Up in the morning's no for me,
Up in the morning early;
When a' the hills are cover'd wi' snaw,
I'm sure it's winter fairly.

Robert Burns

Thaw

Over the land freckled with snow half-thawed
The speculating rooks at their nests cawed
And saw from elm-tops, delicate as flower of grass,
What we below could not see, Winter pass.

Edward Thomas

Twinkle, Twinkle, Planet Blue

A Bright Future?

Twinkle, Twinkle, little Earth,
How I wonder what you're worth.
Chopping forests by the score,
Soon we won't have any more.

Twinkle, Twinkle, planet fair,
What is happening in your air?
Acid rain and airborne lead,
Pretty soon we'll all be dead.

Twinkle, Twinkle, on the sea,
Floating oil and foul debris,
Sewage floating by the shore,
Killing bathers by the score.

Twinkle, Twinkle, planet blue,
Animals are going too.
Chemicals and pesticides,
Causing deaths and suicides.

Twinkle, Twinkle, disco star,
Getting noisier by the bar,
Concorde's roar and jumbo jet,
And it's getting noisier yet!

Twinkle, Twinkle, earthly light,
Glowing brightly in the night.
Caesium, plutonium,
Radon and uranium.

Twinkle, Twinkle, in the sky,
Watch the cruising missiles fly.
Fire a laser, drop a bomb,
Now all the pollution's gone!

Andrew Dawson (aged 12)

One More Battle

Who's that sailor
stern and solemn?
'Tis Lord Nelson
down from his column.

Why goes he limping
up the street?
In search of a long-lost
English Fleet.

Why driven now
to such despair?
The need to breathe
some clean fresh air.

Roger McGough

Baby-K Rap Rhyme

My name is Baby-K
An dis my rhyme
Sit back folks
While I rap my mind;

· Ah rocking with my homegirl,
My Mommy
Ah rocking with my homeboy,
My Daddy
My big sister, Les, an
My Granny,
Hey dere people – my posse
I'm the business
The ruler of the nursery

poop po-doop
poop-poop po-doop
poop po-doop
poop-poop po-doop

Well, ah soaking up de rhythm
Ah drinking up my tea
Ah bouncing an ah rocking
On my Mommy knee
So happy man so happy

poop po-doop
poop-poop po-doop
poop po-doop
poop-poop po-doop

Wish my rhyme wasn't hard
Wish my rhyme wasn't rough
But sometimes, people
You got to be tough

Cause dey pumping up de chickens
Dey stumping down de trees
Dey messing up de ozones
Dey messing up de seas
Baby-K say, stop dis –
please, please, please

poop po-doop
poop-poop po-doop
poop po-doop
poop-poop po-doop

Now am splashing in de bath
With my rubber duck
Who don't like dis rhyme
Kis my baby-foot
Babies everywhere
Join a Babyhood

Cause dey hotting up de globe, man
Dey hitting down de seals
Dey killing off de ellies
for dere ivories
Baby-K say, stop dis –
please, please, please

poop po-doop
poop-poop po-doop
poop po-doop
poop-poop po-doop

Dis is my Baby-K rap
But it's kinda plea
What kinda world
Dey going to leave fuh me?
What kinda world
Dey going to leave fuh me?

  Poop po-doop.

Grace Nichols

Lament of an Arawak Child

Once I played with the hummingbirds
and sang songs to the sea
I told my secrets to the waves
and they told theirs to me.

Now there are no more hummingbirds
the sea's songs are all sad
for strange men came and took this land
and plundered all we had.

They made my people into slaves
they worked us to the bone
they battered us and tortured us
and laughed to hear us groan.

Today we'll take a long canoe
and set sail on the sea
we'll steer our journey by the stars
and find a new country.

Pamela Mordecai

Acid Snow Drops

How deep the snow,
How white it falls,
How cold and sharp the air,
How perfectly each little flake
Pollutes the atmosphere.

Brian Patten

Everything Changes

Everything changes. We plant
trees for those born later
but what's happened has happened,
and poisons poured into the seas
cannot be drained out again.

What's happened has happened.
Poisons poured into the seas
cannot be drained out again, but
everything changes. We plant
trees for those born later.

Cicely Herbert

 **All You Sea**

All You Sea

Three billion gallons
Of sewage
Floating in de sea.
Whales an dolphins
Don't like it,
Seaweed an fish
Don't like it,
De dead at sea
Don't like it,
Zephaniah
Don't like it.

Three billion gallons
Of sewage
Floating in de sea.
There's a time bomb
In our water,
De boats are
Dirty too,
Three billion gallons
Of sewage,
All for you.

Benjamin Zephaniah

The Black Death

I hate oil slicks
that cover the sea,
like a huge tongue that licks
all the living things away,
spreading like a tree . . .

birds with black wings
that struggle and sink,
fish, seals and all the things
that grow in bright colours, deep
black – as black as ink!

Gavin Ewart

Whale

O hear the Whale's
Colossal song!
Suppler than any
Soprano's tongue

And wild as a hand
Among harp strings
Plunging through all
The seas she sings.

Ted Hughes

The Song of the Whale

Heaving mountain in the sea,
Whale, I heard you
Grieving.

Great whale, crying for your life,
Crying for your kind, I knew
How we would use
Your dying:

Lipstick for our painted faces,
Polish for our shoes.

Tumbling mountain in the sea,
Whales, I heard you
Calling.

Bird-high notes, keening, soaring:
At that edge a tiny drum
Like a heartbeat.

We would make you
Dumb.

In the forest of the sea,
Whale, I heard you
Singing,

Singing to your kind.
We'll never let you be.
Instead of life we choose

Lipstick for our painted faces,
Polish for our shoes.

Kit Wright

Whale Poems

(i)   whales
       are floating cathedrals
       let us rejoice

       cavorting mansions
       of joy
       let us give thanks

       divine temples
       of the deep
       we praise thee

(ii)   whaleuja!

(iii)   whalemeat again
       (don't know where
       don't know when

       but I know)
       whalemeat again
       (some sunny day)

(iv)   in the scheme
       of things
       oceanic
       the whale is titanic

       in the
       pecking order
       maritime
       e l e p h a n t i n e

(v) whale :
      my bull

      ocean :
      my corrida

      oilskin :
      my suit of lights

      harpoon :
      my sword of truth

      death :
      my fat purse.

Roger McGough

No Answer

Once the seals had skins
shiny wet as a new anorak.

Now their skins have a rusty look
of an old car part.
The star has fallen out of their eye.

The seals have no answer
to the question
of poisonous waste.

O Laughter
walk on water
that the seals may smile again.

John Agard

maggie and milly and molly and may
went down to the beach (to play one day)

and maggie discovered a shell that sang
so sweetly she couldn't remember her troubles, and

milly befriended a stranded star
whose rays five languid fingers were;

and molly was chased by a horrible thing
which raced sideways while blowing bubbles: and

may came home with a smooth round stone
as small as a world and as large as alone.

For whatever we lose (like a you or a me)
it's always ourselves we find in the sea

e e cummings

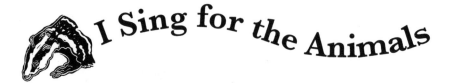# I Sing for the Animals

I Sing for the Animals

Out of the earth
I sing for them,
A Horse nation
I sing for them.
Out of the earth
I sing for them,
The animals
I sing for them.

Native American – Teton Sioux

Hurt No Living Thing

Hurt no living thing;
Ladybird, nor butterfly,
Nor moth with dusty wing,
Nor cricket chirping cheerily,
Nor grasshopper so light of leap,
Nor dancing gnat, nor beetle fat,
Nor harmless worms that creep.

Christina Rossetti

Jamaican Song

Little toad little toad mind yourself
mind yourself let me plant my corn
plant my corn to feed my horse
feed my horse to run my race –
the sea is full of more than I know
moon is bright like night time sun
night is dark like all eyes shut
    Mind – mind yu not harmed
    somody know bout yu
    somody know bout yu

Little toad little toad mind yourself
mind yourself let me build my house
build my house to be at home
be at home till I one day vanish –
the sea is full of more than I know
moon is bright like night time sun
night is dark like all eyes shut
    Mind – mind yu not harmed
    somody know bout yu
    somody know bout yu

James Berry

The Badger

The Badger in the spinney is the true king of this
   land.
All creatures are his tenants, though not all
   understand.

Didicoi red and roe-deer, gypsy foxes, romany
   otters –
They squabble about their boundaries, but all of
   them are squatters.

Even the grandest farm-house, what is it but a
   camp
In the land where the singing Badger walks the
   woods with his hooded lamp?

A farmer's but a blowing seed with a flower of
   crops and herds.
His tractors and his combines are as airy as his
   words.

But the Badger's fort was dug when the whole
   land was one oak.
His face is his ancient coat of arms, and he wears
   the same grey cloak

As if time had not passed at all, as if there were
   no such thing,
As if there were only the one night-kingdom and
   its Badger King.

Ted Hughes

The Red Cockatoo

Sent as a present from Annam –
A red cockatoo.
Coloured like the peach-tree blossom,
Speaking with the speech of men.
And they did to it what is always done
To the learned and eloquent.
They took a cage with stout bars
And shut it up inside.

Anonymous, China,
translated by Arthur Waley

My Mother Saw a Dancing Bear

My mother saw a dancing bear
By the schoolyard, a day in June.
The keeper stood with chain and bar
And whistle-pipe, and played a tune.

And bruin lifted up its head
And lifted up its dusty feet,
And all the children laughed to see
It caper in the summer heat.

They watched as for the Queen it died.
They watched it march. They watched it halt.
They heard the keeper as he cried,
'Now, roly-poly!' 'Somersault!'

And then, my mother said, there came
The keeper with a begging-cup,
The bear with burning coat of fur,
Shaming the laughter to a stop.

They paid a penny for the dance,
But what they saw was not the show;
Only, in bruin's aching eyes,
Far-distant forests, and the snow.

Charles Causley

Chicken Dinner

Mama, don' do it, please,
Don' cook dat chicken fe dinner,
We know dat chicken from she hatch,
She is de only one in de batch
Dat de mongoose didn' catch.
Please don' cook her fe dinner.

Mama, don' do it, please,
Don' cook dat chicken fe dinner,
Yuh mean to tell mi yuh feget
Yuh promise her to we as a pet
She now even have a chance to lay yet
An yuh want to cook her fe dinner.

Mama, don' do it, please,
Don' cook dat chicken fe dinner,
Don' give Henrietta de chop,
Ah tell yuh what, we could swop,
We will get yuh one from de shop,
If yuh promise not to cook her fe dinner.

Mama, me really glad, yuh know,
Yuh never cook Henny fe dinner,
An she glad too, ah bet.
Oh Lawd, me suddenly feel upset,
Yuh don' suppose is somebody else pet
We eating now fe dinner?

Valerie Bloom

The Fighting Temeraire

"THESE BIRDS MUST BE KILLED"
  Headline in the *Angling Times*

I saw a cormorant the other day,
sat on a rock; around him lay
dead anglers – there were nine or ten.
"What's this?" I said. "I'm culling fishermen,"
the bird replied. "I'd thought the sea
was big enough for them as well as me
but no, it seems to be their wish
that I shan't be allowed a single fish.
It's not as if they're likely to go short
at mealtime – they just kill for sport.
And so, if that's the way it's going to be,
from this day on it's either them or me."
And while I stood there pondering what to say,
the cormorant shook his head and flew away

Russell Hoban

Extinction Day

Extinction Day

The Dodo and the Barbary Lion,
The Cuban Yellow Bat,
The Atlas Bear, the Quagga and
The Christmas Island Rat,
The Thylacine, the Blue Buck
And the Hau Kuahiwi plant
Have all one thing in common now,
And that is that they aren't.

Give me one good reason why,
I wonder if you can?
The answer's in a single word –
The word is simply: Man.

Extinction Day, Extinction Day,
It isn't all that far away
For many animals and birds.
So let us decimate the herbs,
Let's hunt their eggs and spoil their land,
Let's give Extinction a Big Hand,
For when it comes, it's here to stay . . .
Extinction Day! Extinction Day!

Terry Jones

Finale for the Animals

Some with cruelty came, sharp-fanged and clawed,
Tore at the air searching for food which, found,
They ate in an instant – new leaves, the tall and small
Flowers. Carnivores were
Worse, hunters of blood, smellers of victims
More miles away than our instruments measure or we
Imagine. Meanwhile the jungle listened and looked.
The parrot kept its beak shut, the slithering snake
Stilled to a coil. The stars were listening, the sun's
Burning paused at the tear and rampage of
A striped or spotted creature. This was the time
Before we were.

Now we have caged and enclosed but not enchanted
Most of these. Now full of power we are not
Gentle with flowers, pull too hard, break the admired
Rose with abandonment. We should know better.

You have heard of the ark and Noah. Most likely it
Was a local event or a myth but remember men
Bow down to the myths they create.
Perhaps we were kindest, most gentle,
Most at our best
When we coupled all creatures and launched them forth in an ark.
Imagination was gracious then indeed,
Gracious too when we thought up the speeding dove,
Feathery emblem of peace whiter than clouds, its wings
Combing and calming the breakers. The waters stilled.
You have heard now of some of these, learnt of their habits.
Do not haunt zoos too often, do not demand
Affection too often from rabbits or cats or dogs,
Do not tame if taming hurts.
Be grateful for such variety of manners,
For the diverse universe.
Above all respect the smallest of all these creatures
As you are awed by the stars.

Elizabeth Jennings

Buffalo Dusk

The buffaloes are gone.
And those who saw the buffaloes are gone.
Those who saw the buffaloes by thousands and how they pawed the
prairie sod into dust with their hoofs, their great heads down
pawing on in a great pageant of dusk,
Those who saw the buffaloes are gone.
And the buffaloes are gone.

Carl Sandburg

Ice Bears

"Polar bears face extinction and a large number of
other animals will be reduced to tiny remnant
populations by global warming in the Arctic regions,
the World Wide Fund says in a report today."

News story by Paul Brown,
The Guardian, 17 December 1996

Huge, silent-moving like
white dreams hungering for
the yester-prey,
what will they do when
the ice is gone?

Will they move south, wear
brightly-coloured sports shirts,
drink Coca-Cola?

Will they sleep in
cardboard boxes, beg for
small change?

Or will they, knowing how
things end, swim on
and on and on
into the darkness
when the ice is gone?

Russell Hoban

Christmas Wise

All I **want** fe christmas is world peace
I **don't want** loads a food dat I really can't eat
All I **want** fe christmas is a long holiday
An a house in Jamaica where I can stay.
I **don't want** kisses under mistletoe from
Sloppy people I don't know,
I **won't** be putting out nu stocking cos
I **don't** wear de tings,
I **won't** be cutting down nu christmas trees,
I like dem living.

All I **want** fe christmas is dis planet for ever
Fully complete wid its ozone layer
All I **want** fe christmas is friends and . . .
No more records from Status Quo,
I **don't want** a white christmas an I bet
We'll get nu more of dem cos of de Greenhouse effect,
An I **reckon** at christmas we create too much waste
Maybe a green christmas is more to my taste.
All I **want** fe christmas is sum honesty
About de wisdom of christmas
An how it should be
all I **want** fe christmas is clean air,
but I reckon I won't get none

Benjamin Zephaniah

Space Dog Remembers

First dog in orbit
and proud of it.
But was scared, must admit

Felt trapped
in a kennel of air.
My cry lost among a million spheres.

Kept wishing every minute
Would return to earth soon.
Couldn't bring myself to bark at moon.

No dog smell among the clouds.
No ball to chase. No stick.
What's the good wagging at a planet?

My paws longed for sand or grass.
Preferred the park to a sputnik.
But raised my hind legs out of habit.

Return to earth was the best bit.
Was given marvellous doggie biscuit.
My picture on every front page.

Now in paw-licking old age
I ask myself, was it worth it?

But I am man's best friend.
On earth, on moon, wherever
I will wag his welcome to the end.

I have a home.
I have a bone.
A tale to tell.

John Agard

Elephant

If I could be reincarnated
   (And who knows, I might have been already?)
Then I'd like to return as an elephant
   Reliable and steady.

Big as a room filled with sunshine,
   A giant, gentle and strong,
Lord of the manor
   I'd roam the savannah
Trumpeting all day long.

At sunset it's down to the river
   To meet my old pals for a chat
After a few bouts of trunk-wrestling
   We'd squirt water, do daft things like that.

Then tired and happy we'd lumber home
   Humming an elephant tune
Thinking our thanks to our maker
   By the light of an elephant moon.

If I could be reincarnated
   An elephant I would choose,
Failing that, Napoleon,
   Kim Basinger or Ted Hughes.

Roger McGough

Elephant Eternity

Elephants walking under juicy-leaf trees
Walking with their children under juicy-leaf trees
Elephants elephants walking like time

Elephants bathing in the foam-floody river
Fountaining their children in the mothery river
Elephants elephants bathing like happiness

    Strong and gentle elephants
    Standing on the earth
    Strong and gentle elephants
    Like peace

Time is walking under elephant trees
Happiness is bathing in the elephant river
Strong gentle peace is shining
All over the elephant earth

Adrian Mitchell

Enjoy the Earth Gently

Blowin' in the Wind

How many roads must a man walk down
Before yu call him a man?
Yes, 'n how many seas must a white dove sail
Before she sleeps in the sand?
Yes, 'n how many times must the cannon balls fly
Before they're forever banned?
The answer, my friend, is blowin' in the wind,
The answer is blowin' in the wind.

How many times must a man look up
Before he can see the sky?
Yes, 'n how many ears must one man have
Before he can hear people cry?
Yes, 'n how many deaths will it take till he knows
That too many people have died?
The answer, my friend, is blowin' in the wind,
The answer is blowin' in the wind.

How many years can a mountain exist
Before it's washed to the sea?
Yes, 'n how many years can some people exist
Before they're allowed to be free?
Yes, 'n how many times can a man turn his head,
Pretending he just doesn't see?
The answer, my friend, is blowin' in the wind,
The answer is blowin' in the wind.

Bob Dylan

Shadows

Lovely the shadows
of gulls at rest on the water

of trout hovering over sunlit gravel
in the river

of the oak at sunset
lengthening down the hill

Different the shadows

that darken the chart

fill the window

stop the heart.

Robert Hull

Silver

Slowly, silently, now the moon
Walks the night in her silver shoon;
This way, and that, she peers, and sees
Silver fruit upon silver trees;
One by one the casements catch
Her beams beneath the silver thatch;
Couched in his kennel, like a log,
With paws of silver sleeps the dog;
From their shadowy cote the white breasts peep
Of doves in a silver-feathered sleep;
A harvest mouse goes scampering by,
With silver claws and silver eye;
And moveless fish in the water gleam,
By silver reeds in a silver stream.

Walter de la Mare

Daybreak

The curtains of the solemn night
    Draw back; and daybreak fair
Shines on these tulips cold with dew,
    And fills with light the air.
No child stands tiptoe yet to sip
Clear water from the fountain's lip;
    Nothing stirs anywhere,
But the birds in the dust, the leaves in the breeze,
The nut-brown squirrels in the trees;
    And empty is every chair.

Walter de la Mare

from **The Tempest**

Be not afeard. The isle is full of noises,
Sounds, and sweet airs, that give delight and hurt not.
Sometimes a thousand twangling instruments
Will hum about mine ears; and sometime voices
That if I then had waked after long sleep
Will make me sleep again; and then in dreaming
The clouds methought would open, and show riches
Ready to drop upon me, that when I waked
I cried to dream again.

The Tempest, Act III, Scene ii
William Shakespeare

Pippa's Song

The year's at the spring;
The day's at the morn;
Morning's at seven;
The hillside's dew-pearled;
The lark's on the wing;
The snail's on the thorn;
God's in His heaven –
All's right with the world!

Robert Browning

Enjoy the earth gently
Enjoy the earth gently
For if the earth is spoiled
It cannot be repaired
Enjoy the earth gently

from the oral tradition of the Yoruba People

Index of first lines

Acknowledgements

The editor and publisher would like to thank the following for permission to reproduce poems:

'No Answer' from *Laughter is an Egg*, by kind permission of John Agard c/o Caroline Sheldon Literary Agency, published by Puffin Books; 'Space Dog Remembers' from *We Animals Want a Word with You*, by kind permission of John Agard c/o Caroline Sheldon Literary Agency, published by Red Fox; 'Haiku '2' 'Haiku Moments 3' from *Playing a Dazzler* by James Berry (Hamish Hamilton, 1996) copyright © James Berry, 1996, reproduced by permission of Hamish Hamilton Ltd; 'Jamaican Song' from *When I Dance* by James Berry (Hamish Hamilton, 1988), reprinted by permission of the Peters, Fraser and Dunlop Group Limited on behalf of James Berry; 'My Mother Saw a Dancing Bear' from *Collected Poems* by Charles Causley (Macmillan); 'The Village Shop' © Gillian Clarke, by permission of the author; 'I Had a Little Piece of Earth' from *First Rhymes* by Lucy Coates, first published in the UK by Orchard Books, a division of the Watts Publishing Group, London; 'Pine Forest' by Wendy Cope by permission of the author; 'The Prayer of the Little Bird' from *Prayers from the Ark* by Carmen Bernos de Gasztold (Macmillan); 'Daybreak' and 'Silver' from *The Complete Poems of Walter de la Mare*, 1969 (USA, 1970), by permission of the Literary Trustees of Walter de la Mare and the Society of Authors as their representative; 'The Rainflower' from *The Word Party* by Richard Edwards (Lutterworth, 1986); 'The Black Death' from *Like It or Not* by Gavin Ewart (Bodley Head, 1992), reproduced by permission of Mrs Margaret Ewart; 'Autumn Sigheth' from *The Children's Bells* by Eleanor Farjeon (Oxford University Press); 'The Fighting Temeraire' and 'Ice Bears' from *The Last of the Wallendas* by Russell Hoban (Hodder & Stoughton); 'April Rain Song' from *Collected Poems* by Langston Hughes copyright © 1994 by the Estate of Langston Hughes, reprinted by permission of Alfred A. Knopf Inc; 'Shadows' from *Stargazer* by Robert Hull, reproduced by permission of Hodder & Stoughton; 'Finale for the Animals' from *A Spell of Words* by Elizabeth Jennings (Macmillan); 'Extinction Day' by Terry Jones from *The Curse of the Vampire's Socks*, reprinted by permission of Pavilion Books; 'Oxleas Wood' from *Two's Company* by Jackie Kay (Blackie, 1992) copyright © Jackie Kay, 1992, reproduced by permission of Penguin Books Ltd; 'Trees are Great' from *Pillow Talk*, 'One More Battle' and 'Elephant' from *Bad Bad Cats* (Viking, 1997), 'Morning Has Broken' from *Lucky* (Viking, 1993) and 'Whale Poems' from *Sky in the Pie* by Roger McGough, all © Roger McGough and reprinted by permission of the Peters, Fraser and Dunlop Group Limited on behalf of Roger McGough; 'I Have an Oasis' from *There's*